Buck Journeys to Martha's Vineyard

Becky Cross Saganich

*with Illustrations
by J. Stephen Moyle*

Perspective Books, LLC
Shirley, Massachusetts

I dedicate this book to

Andrew Jacob Weaver

whose brief life changed my own.

First in the **Life's Perspectives Series**
Editors: Charles Tellier and Alfred Yesue
Design and Color: Becky Cross Saganich
Composition: Boynton Hue Studio

Library of Congress Card Number: 00-105339

ISBN 0-9701736-01

Printed in the United States of America

00 01 02 03 4 3 2 1

In 1898 a little house was made,
Set up in a city midst houses making shade.
It sat through one whole winter, empty and alone,
Hoping one day someone would want it for a home.
My grandfather was working for the man who owned the place.
They both agreed it'd be better off at a Martha's Vineyard pace.

So the house was moved from Worcester, by wagon, train, and ship.
My grandfather, the new owner, was looking forward to the trip.
The house was set and ready for my family to move right in,
So they sent their things ahead of them, 'til summer did begin.

So there it sits, it's changed a bit, over the many years.
It's real all right, it's a simple sight, but we welcome it with cheers.
So read along with Mom or Dad, sister, friend, or brother.
Our house's story here unfolds. It's unlike any other.

1

Once there was a little house on a quiet street in the city of Worcester, Massachusetts. It was a special kind of house made of large panels hung on hinges, making it easy to put together. The house was ordered from a catalog and shipped by train to Worcester. Men came, put the house together, and finished it with a fresh coat of paint. It was a happy little house with only two rooms, a small porch on the front, and a shed on the back. The little house's name was Buck. Buck lived in a neighborhood with many homes filled with families. He was particularly fond of the children and wondered how long it would be before he would have a family of his own.

Time passed, and still
Buck remained empty. One
day a family came to visit. They
seemed to like him very much. A little boy
and his younger sister ran through each room
opening and closing all of his windows. They explored
every nook and cranny, tickling Buck's insides. It was fun being a
part of their game. But their fun was short-lived, and in no time at all he
was alone again. He wondered if this family would be the one he was hoping
for. He waited patiently. Days and weeks passed, but the family did not return.

Winter came and covered Buck in a blanket of white snow. He felt cold and lonely. During the day Buck watched neighborhood children playing, while at night, their warmly lit homes smelled of wonderful things. Buck longed for the happy sounds and warmth of his own family and wondered if he would always be alone.

4

In time, the cold snows of winter melted away. The coming of spring renewed Buck's hope for a family. The sun warmed his shingles and took the chill out of his hinges. Being a poet at heart, and feeling inspired by spring, Buck thought up a poem to remember the day.

Springtime

When springtime comes
The chill has gone;
Opening snowdrops
With the dawn.

She warms the birds
Who nest in the trees,
And graces flowers
A-buzz with bees.

Umbrellas pop up
Beneath her rain
Like little rooftops,
Dark and plain.

She nurtures it all,
Including each bloom
During the months
From March to June.

Yet, just as she wafted
In on a breeze,
Her exit is subtle,
Canopied by . . . trees.

Early one spring morning, a team of men arrived with their tools and two horse drawn wagons. The men began to carefully take the little house apart. Buck was uneasy, but as long as his hinges weren't damaged, he knew that he could easily be put back together. The factory where Buck had been made constructed lots of houses that were simple to put together and take apart.

6

After several hours Buck was a pile of lumber tied onto the wagons with great leather straps. His windows were carefully removed and wrapped in special moving blankets to protect them from being broken. Buck was very uncomfortable.

With everything secure, the wagons slowly made their way through the quiet, tree-lined streets of Worcester. Buck remembered his trip by train from the factory and hoped he would go by train again.

It was a short ride to Union Station. The wagons stopped in the freight yard where Buck was loaded onto a flatcar and left to wait on a siding. The station echoed with the sounds and rhythms of people and trains hard at work. Great engines with their smokestacks billowing were coupled to long trains loaded with heavy freight. Engineers checked their engines as trainmen checked their switches and signals. Passengers purchased tickets and conductors called out, "Alllll Abooaard!" It was all so exciting! The commotion in the station seemed to have a rhythm of its own and inspired him once more.

The Commotion of Train Motion

Freight cars bump and engines pull.
That car's empty; this one's full.
Clickity clack, rumble, rumble,
All aboard and here we go!

Trainmen's whistles call out loud.
Steam puffs out in a great big cloud.
Clickity clack, rumble, rumble,
All aboard and here we go!

Clocks are chiming; tracks are humming.
"Are you going? Are you coming?"
Clickity clack, rumble, rumble,
All aboard and here we go!

"Buy your tickets; get them here."
"Please don't dawdle; it's time my dear."
Clickity clack, rumble, rumble,
All aboard and **Here We GO!**

Buck liked being in the train station, but once the sun went down, he quickly fell fast asleep.

9

Early the next morning Buck awoke with a loud blast from the engine's whistle. The stationmaster signaled the "all clear" and the train began to move. Buck was both excited and nervous, for although most houses never get to travel, this was his **second** trip on a train.

It didn't take long for the city to disappear and for the train to pass through the low-lying hills of the country.

The train passed through many towns, some BIG and some small. At each station, passengers got on and off as freight was unloaded and replaced with new. Children often chased the train out of the stations, laughing as they played. Seeing the children made Buck sad. He remembered the children in Worcester and wondered if any would ever play within his walls again.

By noon the train reached the top of Buzzards Bay and crossed a bridge onto Cape Cod. At first Buck thought this part of the country looked quite plain. There were very few trees, and without them Buck quivered from the strong sea breeze. Nonetheless, when the wind blew, the marshes moved gently like waves on the ocean. Spring by the shore isn't as green as it is inland, but it has a beauty all its own.

The train arrived in the port of Woods Hole late in the afternoon. It is here that trains meet ships from up and down the coast carrying passengers and freight bound for the islands of Martha's Vineyard and Nantucket. Once Buck's train came to a full stop, the passengers quickly gathered their belongings, got off, and boarded an awaiting steamer. With one long toot from its whistle, the boat pulled away from the dock and headed out onto Vineyard Sound. Buck imagined what it would be like to be a passenger and thought up a poem.

Passenger's Tale

Gather up your belongings; its time to get going,
The train ride is over. The excitement is growing.
Being a passenger riding the train,
We just want to get there, sunshine or rain.

Out on the platform collecting our things,
The engine pulls out as the steamer bell rings.
Being a passenger off the train now,
It's the first time for some; others know how.

We paid for our tickets. Let's check where we put them.
The steamer is waiting. We'll need to produce them.
Being a passenger, first train car, now ship,
The first half is over, let's get on with our trip!